MENDING HOLES

MENDING HOLES

Patrick Dixon

MoonPath Press

Copyright © 2025 Patrick Dixon

All rights reserved.
No part of this publication may be reproduced, distributed, or transmitted in any form or by any means whatsoever without written permission from the publisher, except in the case of brief excerpts for critical reviews and articles. All inquiries should be addressed to MoonPath Press.

Poetry
ISBN 979-8-9899488-2-6

Cover photo: Patrick Dixon

Author photo: Veronica Kessler

Book design: Tonya Namura, using
Minion Pro (text) and Gill Sans (display).

MoonPath Press, an imprint of Concrete Wolf Poetry Series, is dedicated to publishing the finest poets living in the U.S. Pacific Northwest.

MoonPath Press
c/o Concrete Wolf
PO Box 2220
Newport, OR 97365-0163

MoonPathPress@gmail.com

http://MoonPathPress.com

for Veronica

Log

Sextant	3
A Blessing for the Fishermen	5
Slack Tide	6
Praise Alaska	7
Boat Puller	9
Fishing Gesture	10
Rain Dream	12
Middle Rip, Cook Inlet	14
Ransom	17
Payback	19
Other Fishing Jobs	20
Waiting to Deliver	21
The Bucket	24
Some Fourth of Julys	26
Overboard	28
Boat Fire	30
What Lingers	32
Sharp Knife	34
Speck	35
A Fishing Love Poem	37
Twilight on the Boat	39
Pompadour	41
Under the Curve	44
Farewell	46
Buoys	49
The Old Man and the Sea Deal	50
It's Never the First	52
Dust	54

Summer's Ebb	56
Where'd All the Fish Go?	58
Snuffy	60
Flash in the Distance	61
First Net	62
I Have a Question	64
Fat City in Four Directions	66
Microphone	68
View from the Stern	70
Mending Holes	72
Writing About Fishing	74
Exit Strategy	75
Acknowledgments	77
Gratitude	79
About the Author	81

MENDING HOLES

Sextant

*for John Bird, inventor, astronomer,
mathematician, 1757*

Stand at the rail, lift mystery to eye
(you only need one to calculate latitude),

fix sun at solar noon, Polaris at apex,
or sight the moon. Dance with her

on a darkening sea. You will know
where you stand as you float. How many

fathoms lie beneath your feet? The watch
you began will indeed end. Salt air dries in

your nostrils. The ship's bell rings once, twice,
eight times; rolls over waves, across lines

of demarcation. We engrave our names on iron
gongs. There is irony in yours, *Bird*—who gifted

navigation to those who couldn't sense it
internally so we might find our mathematic

feathered way. Wings spread, we hold course
in an oak and brass instrument. Adjust

for error, for the height of eye above sea level.
Or was it heart? Be sure to add the distance from

surface to the deck—include the thickness of your boots.
Pluck a star from the sky. Place it on a mirrored

horizon. Day or night, you will know
where you are in time, while the rest of us

are left with only enough angle to see water.

A Blessing for the Fishermen

To the gods who do not care,
indifferent to our feeble desires,
please just for a moment, listen:

calm your waves,
unbundle your clouds,
hold your winds.

Let fish come and let fish go.
Let the work tire them,
make them ache for home.

Above all, spare them.
Grant them passage.
Send them back.

Slack Tide

I arrive at the shore
in time for the long moment
when seas pause, fingers
outstretched for the moon.
The spell calms the water's rush,
pauses the insistent current.

This sleeping giant
I live upon has rolled over
and stopped breathing.
I hold my breath too,
arctic tern, wings
folded for the dive,
waiting for the exhale.

Praise Alaska

Praise the 1,500 miles of gravel I drove,
praise the windshield, shattered by rocks,
lap sprayed with broken glass. Praise
mountains walked, tents pitched,
camp coffee and the .44 on my hip.

Praise endless summer light. Praise swift glacial
rivers threading turquoise through broad gravel beds.
Praise the abundant North Pacific, home to Beluga,
Humpback, Gray, Bowhead, Orca. Praise each fish
my nets caught and all they let pass. Praise my boats,
how they floated even when they didn't run. Praise
baked salmon, grilled salmon, kippered salmon,
salmon jerky, smoked salmon, salmonberries, lowbush,
highbush, bog blueberries, glistening currant.
Praise the bears that ate them first.

Praise the hurried race from breakup to termination dust.
Praise winter's chill, hoarfrost, 30 below and silent snow.
Praise the howl of wolves across the valley. Praise the
gangly moose, head dipped beneath water, mouth
streaming lily pads. Praise the caribou crossing
ice-burdened rivers, dodging floes headed out
with the tide. Praise the giant tides.

Praise the white cloud clatter of snow geese rising
from the flats. Praise the chortle of the sandhill,
flight impossibly high under a midnight sun.
Praise the eagle's chitter atop the spruce.
Praise raven's rasp and croak. Praise totems
and masks. Praise all who came before, from
Native to Russian to cheechako to sourdough.
Praise wilderness, the silence of woods.
Praise the arctic breeze, praise, oh praise

the warm Chinook wind, the forget-me-not,
the lupine, the fireweed-filled meadows.

Praise nights wrapped
in sleeping bag and blanket cocoons,
stars streaking behind green
curtains of northern lights.

Praise the years I spent.
Praise the days to come.

Boat Puller

for Jim

We were alone on the boat—
a green deckhand and a middle-aged Norwegian
riding emerald rollers sprinkled with drops of gold
in the late afternoon sun.
And though you were teaching me
how to get a salmon out of the bag
without popping the mesh,
   I was somewhere else:

off the stern I saw myself
neck deep in Indiana, foundering in all those years
of not knowing who I was or how to escape
who I had become; drowning in aching nights
spent hoping for the moment I might know
   a way to set my feet upon a path of my own.

While I was picking fish with you,
stunned at the sight of the sea so near
and the mountains filling the western sky,
I thought of dry Midwestern cornfields,
and of lost, empty days filled with a wish to leave
   but nowhere to go.

You bent over a red to show me how to use a fish pick,
never realizing what was happening to me,
how you were stripping away the web of my past life,
   pulling me through to solid ground.

Fishing Gesture

I stand in the stern, holding a line and a bright orange buoy attached to our net spooled onto the reel next to me. My skipper is in the cabin on the radio. I can hear voices of other fishermen in our group, barking excited static from deck speakers: *Three in the air at once! Fish everywhere! Looks better a little south of me.*

I watch for jumpers and wonder at this fishing enterprise I'm engaged in. In minutes, hundreds of us will cast our nets into the skin of the planet, fishing a surface sliver of deeper water to catch salmon swimming there. In their frenzy to return to the river of their birth and spawn, schools of them have risen from the depths under us and seem to want to fly the rest of the way home.

Our boat idles in the choppy sea, drifting. I wait with building anxiety. What if they move past us? What if the tide takes us out of the school? What if another boat pulls in just south of us and corks us off? What if…

I notice the boat closest to us. We are far enough apart to be out of each other's way when we set the gear, but I see my counterpart on the other vessel, standing in the picking well, waiting like me, and my mind lifts…

§

I am above the fleet, seeing deckhand after deckhand, each holding a buoy, waiting for the surge of the throttle and the skipper's shout, *Let 'er go!*

The boats lurch forward, and together we toss the moment into the air; hundreds of bright orange buoys soar through morning light in fluid motion, like salmon leap to return to water, weightless, fishing air for the sea. The noise of engines recedes as the fishing gesture echoes its way into the past, connecting all these tossed nets to all other nets ever thrown into the ocean. We have done this before, not always like this, but always *like this*, with an arc of net and line lacing its way through the sky to the water, to the fish, to the planet.

Rain Dream

I stand in oilskins on the flying bridge, looking over the bow.
Raindrops sting my face as the boat slices
through the ocean swell. Soundless circles dance
on the side of a glassy wave, expand then disappear
into the ripples of newer drops—light upon dark upon light,
a silent ballet in a world filled with more urgent noises.

The swell rolls past. I arise at anchor to a muted patter
on the roof of the boat. Barely audible, the rain utters
a gentle whisper I might understand, if I listen hard enough.

I try. I slip outside into a soft downpour of voices
I have never before encountered. In the predawn light
I watch tiny liquid explosions on a gray mirror of ocean.
The boats of the fleet, dull and oblivious, sway
on their anchors in the near distance, dark gray forms
against lighter grays of water and cloud, all connected,
shrouded, washed in rain.

The sound of hissing is faint. At first I don't hear it under
the thrum of drops on the deck, pings on the metal mast,
plops off the rigging, off the gunwales into the sea.
All that is more conscious, more lucid. Underneath
is a lighter, softer white noise. It is as if the sea and sky
are conversing in a foreign tongue—a language so primal
as to be all but inaudible to my modern ear filled as it is
with sounds I not only help create, but inspire.

Buddha speaks of seeking silence—an inner peace
that is heart and soul of existence. For a few moments
standing on deck, for a few heartbeats floating
on a calm sea, I eavesdrop upon another dimension.
I sway heavily on an anchor of my own, hooked deep,
listening to forces engulf me like an ocean.

§

The rain eases, the clouds lift, the sky brightens.
I blink away the reverie, notice fat raindrops dripping
from the bill of my cap. A chill from my soaked socks
raises the hair on the back of my neck. I turn and open
the cabin door—it's time to turn up the stove
and brew hot coffee with water that fell from the sky.

Middle Rip, Cook Inlet

It has been cloudy now
a long, long while.
The sea is building.
The unexpected blow
comes from the south,
and is always the worst.

From shore you can't see
the middle rip;
can't tell how bad it is—
waves crashing in all directions at once,
moving mountains of green and gray.

And even if you were there
fighting the wheel to keep her on course,
quartering them up and over, throttle forward
and back, watching more of what's next
than what's now, you couldn't tell whether
the changing tide would lay it down
or stir it up more.

I've run away from the middle rip
more than once: turned around, saying,
    This is unfishable!
Gritted my teeth, hung on to the helm as the boat
swung in the trough, trying to time it so the smallest wave
was the one that hit; watched out the side window,
wishing we would turn faster—knowing we couldn't,
braced as the wave slammed the side like a sledgehammer.
Watched hats, silverware, coffee cups, magazines, camera
and books slide in synchrony across dash and galley table,
reach the edge and erupt around the cabin.

I've even set my gear in the middle rip
with a groan as it kicked up, thinking
    Ahh, it'll come down.
I've seen my deckhand crouch
on the back deck, holding on as the boat heeled,
trying to let the net out without a hang-up,
with a glance over his shoulder
and a look that asked *Are you insane?*

And I have stared dumbly out the cabin door
at towering waves behind him, stern
lifting toward vertical, thinking
    Yes. Yes I am.

It's not so bad fishing the middle rip,
but towing the gear in heavy weather
depends upon your mettle and your nerve;
and you know you've got to pick up:
pull your hat down hard so it doesn't blow off,
put on oilskins and button the top button
no matter how tight. The cool press of raingear
against your neck reminds you of how much
you wish you didn't have to go out there
into the wind and rollers and make
the boat go stern-first into them.

You open the cabin door, and the wind
tries to take your breath, but you suck it back,
clench your jaw, hold the lifeline and dance
down the deck, timing it so the side you're on
lifts away from the water as you move aft.

You pull on gloves as you eye the seas
from the stern of your boat—your boat,
your machine, full of warmth, life
and power to pull in all that net

stretching into the hostile gray glare
until you can't see it any longer—
and your boat can get it all back, and more:
she can deliver you safely home.

And it's you and your boat against all this
space, wind and water. You come alive,
stomp your foot on the treadle, and the reel
whines, turns and backs the boat
into the waves. The sea slaps the stern
like an insult, drenching you in ice water.
You duck, come up sputtering, laugh,
whoop, and yell the insult back at the sea!

From shore you can't see
the middle rip;
can't tell how bad it is.

Ransom

Boat work in four parts

      1
Balance on elbow in yoga-crab pose,
stretch under floorboards
in the engine room, between the batteries
and the transducer post. Commit your weight
until the wrench pops free—punch of skin
and cartilage left on the starter motor—
another pre-season blood sacrifice.

The High Druid of Engines chants obscenities
as you rise and dance, reciting lines
from a waterborne play. Comedy? Tragedy?
You don't know the difference,
except the boat's not in the water.
That comes later, after your hands are
scabbed and tattooed in black grease.
Salt water will cleanse you. Until then,
bag balm stings the cuts, and the older
you are the more the knuckles ache.

      2
Blood burns your eyes,
dripping off the gash in your forehead
cracked on the prop blade under the boat.
Stunned, you drop on all fours to the gravel.
No dance when it hurts this bad. Just the swearing.
Thick blurred pearls slide off the end of your nose,
land black among stones, red on the back of your hand.

      3
The one day you don't wear gloves,
your hand slips against the edge of a sheet of plywood.

The pressed wood puckers,
kisses a one-inch wooden sliver
into the meat of your palm.
That'll leave a mark,
says the smart-ass shipwright.
If you weren't hopping around so much
you'd smack him with the ball-peen.

4

Stumble home through woods—
2:00 am, drunk from the bar. Spruce
root flips you, drops you face-first
into a log peppered with broken branches.
The image in the morning-after mirror
has bruises blossoming around the scabs.

The season is around the next bend,
if you can just stay in the channel.
Scars fade in the waning light
of boat work. Cast off. Salt water
cools your hands on the mooring line,
your dreams no longer held ransom.

Payback

There are parts of this
I don't talk about, face,
admit. Sleepless nights,
house shuddering in wind
before a fish day, eyes open
on the ceiling, out the window,
wondering beyond bad water,
pounding rollers and my own
helplessness. *Have I done this
before? Drowned in a past life?*
What else explains this loss of rational
thought; payment for mistakes ended under
water? I thought selling out would remedy the
fear. It did. But my son goes fishing this spring
and I am awake in bed again, listening.

Other Fishing Jobs

for Dylan, 2015

Tell your daughter you love her
so often she'll remember.
Tell your mother, too.

Watch the sun rise over the ocean.
Notice how slow it goes,
how much is packed into

the hour before dawn.
Do it until you understand
what daybreak means.

Call home. Often. Even when
you're so tired you can't think
of anything to say.

On the boat, hold on. Keep a firm
conscious grip on the rail—
never trust the sea.

Remember each day with your heart,
then camera, pen, head. You will only feel
like this once. Write letters to your daughter

so she'll know what this meant to you—
why you left. Mail them when you reach port.
Make sure whoever gets them knows to save them

for when she's old enough.

Waiting to Deliver

On the good day
when boats return home
low in the water, holds full,
nets wrapped around salmon
rolled on the reel,

after picking half the net,
and laying it back out
while the fish keep hitting,
then running to the other end
and doing it again, all day long—

no time for breaks, a sandwich
or even water, your face, beard
and glasses streaked black by gurry,
dotted white with scales, back
aching, fingers and wrists sore,

you find energy reserves—
threads of adrenaline buried deep
sustain you 'til you've made the run home
and toss a line to the boat you tie behind,
the last of a dozen hanging off the port stern

next to a matching group tied
to the starboard side of the tender
taking fish anchored in the middle
of the river. This day of donkeywork,
this day of absolution isn't over,

won't be for hours. At the back
of the queue, you know you'll be here
past dinner, past dark, maybe past dawn.
You'll eat a baked potato and a red salmon
garnished with lemon, onion and butter

less than two hours from the time
you plucked it alive from the sea.
You'll wash it down with a cold beer
from the cooler, watch the sunset
and think how this is the best,

most complete life you can imagine.
Salt air cools as shadows lengthen
and the water changes from blue to black.
You trade bunk time with your deckhand
and fall asleep before your head

hits the pillow. The smack of a boathook
on the bow wakes you both as the next
boat in line cuts you all loose to go deliver
and those of you still tethered together
like a serpent in the glare of arc lights

work to move up—fighting the current,
pulled and yanked off course by boats
fore and aft, bumping throttles forward,
neutral, reverse, trying not to ram the one
ahead of you, hoping the one behind you

does the same. Your deckhand fends off
as you swing too close to the vessels sleeping
to starboard, until the lead boat tosses
a line around the tender's cleat again
and you all slide back in the current like a sigh.

Engine after engine goes silent, lines creak
around the cleats as they stretch taut.
Your crew slips into the bunk while you
settle back in the skipper's chair,
light a smoke and sip a cold cup of coffee.

You're still waiting. Waiting to deliver.

The Bucket

All the years I've been on a boat,
commercial fishin' on the ocean afloat,
I always seemed to find a way to be
what you might call hygienic—
and never use a bucket at sea.

Now let me explain—my first job was as a crew
on a Cook Inlet gillnetter—and I was new,
so I worked hard and kept my mouth shut
when given all the crappiest jobs, but
all this business with work boats and fish,
the hardest thing to stomach was the dish
my skipper fed me when he said with a smile,
like he knew just how I'd react all the while:
There ain't no toilet on a boat, it's called a 'head'.
We ain't got one here, so use that there bucket instead.

The container he pointed to was black and thin,
tucked behind the ladder, it barely had a rim.
I found out later some guys have a toilet seat
they put on their bucket to make it complete.
But the sketchiest thing was—I mean, what the heck?
I'd have to use it where we pick fish, on the back deck?
Wherever we fished there were other boats around;
seemed to me the only privacy was back on solid ground
or in the head of another boat that might tie up for a while—
where I could close a door and do my work in solitary style.
No, I was convinced, but didn't show it or say it out loud,
there was no way I was performing in front of a crowd!

So I held it—sometimes for days.
And I never really relinquished my restricted ways.
When we were at sea or even anchored up—
didn't matter for how long—I was one bound-up pup!

With a nod toward the bucket, my skipper once said,
Don't you EVER take a sit?
Not on THIS boat! I shot back, and turned my head to spit.
Well, how do you do that when we been fishin' for days?
he asked, and shook his head at my unnatural ways.
I have a strong sphincter, I began… *Ya see—ah, chuck it!*
I'm telling you I'll never use that stinkin' ol' bucket!
I won't have turds slosh about when the weather gets rough
and slap my port and starboard as we roll in the trough!
And what if that flimsy sucker collapses under me
when I'm sittin' out there emptyin' my scuppers at sea?
I'm tellin' you, skip, I have a fishhold full of motivation
for me to maintain this extensive constipation!
And I intend on holdin' it 'til the season's over and done,
when I can pull down my raingear and rest my bum
on a nice, white toilet seat above a clean porcelain bowl—
where I can properly deposit…a civilized roll!

That said, we went back to work,
and though I was full of it, I tried to not be a jerk.
But whenever a boat with a head tied alongside,
I'd start to feel the surge of an outgoing, ebbing tide!
And when we hit the dock, it was always a lively chase
as off the boat I'd fly and to the cannery john I'd race!
I know my skipper on more than one occasion
wagered a bet against me, but the rising sensation
inside me of impending jet propulsion
always seemed to result in a positive conclusion.
I always made it! I'm really not sure how;
but my sphincter and legs kept my stern clean somehow.

I'll fly my flag high: I'm proud to say I always did duck it,
and never, ever, ever used that old black bucket!

Some Fourth of Julys

found us rafted up in Snug Harbor
drinking Cuervo and beer,
cooking crab caught on rings over the side,
and hoping the weather held
through the next fishing period.

War was the furthest thing from our minds.

In those days the first Gulf War hadn't happened yet,
and far from newspapers, televisions and radios
was why we were there at all.
Emery would arrange to have a keg delivered
by float plane. He'd throw it on a cart,
tow it up the beach with a four-wheeler,
and drop it in a hole filled with cannery ice
near a pile of pallets the size of a setnet skiff.

We'd head to shore for showers at the cannery
and the faint hope a good-looking deckhand
might be available this year.
We'd light the bonfire in the dim light
of a midsummer Alaskan evening.
No one cared if you were Republican or Democrat.
Only Emery was upset if you fished for another outfit
and were drinking his company beer.
But if you were dry, there was always
someone drunk enough to sneak you a cup.

The boats with kids on them would launch bottle rockets,
and some asshole would toss firecrackers into the fire.
We'd all jump and laugh and raise our cups.
Though I can't recall anyone saying it,
it was the Fourth of July all right,

and standing on the shores of a wild land
far from the cares of politics and civilization,
we were all about celebrating our freedom.

Until one year, as the fire burned low
and people drifted toward their bunks,
a few of us lingered, not wanting the night to end.
A fisherman named Harold stood on the deck
of the boat he'd run onto the gravel beach,
and opened fire at the sky with an automatic rifle.

Someone said later it was an Uzi;
I don't know if it was, but we all jumped
as it belched flames three feet long into the black night
and sent hundreds of sleeping kittiwakes
screaming into the sky.
The sound was such a surprise
and the light was so bright
no one thought about the bullets.

It was a long moment inside that noise.
When it ended our eyes ached and our ears rang.
Harold yelled something muffled
and strutted into his cabin.
The rest of us stood there and tried to understand
what we'd just seen.

   Jesus, said a voice next to me.

I thought for a long time about the fact that somebody
actually had a machine gun in his boat
on the fishing grounds.

The bonfires and the kegs stopped after that.
The wars hadn't even started.

Overboard

for Jeff and Debi

It was a cannery truck, we said afterward.
Unreliable. It would stall when he slowed down.
He probably coasted through the stop sign.

Bone cancer doesn't relent, the doctors told her.
Go. Live. Enjoy the time you have left.
For five years she did exactly that:
dove the Great Barrier Reef,
went to China,
fished the lake behind her cabin with her niece.
When she was done,
she slipped away overnight.

It doesn't take much—
a gentle roll of the boat as the wake
passes; the brush of an elbow
and the power drill, set too close to the edge,
tips and tumbles overboard.
You see it roll: watch without
moving, frozen in a dream.
It doesn't even complete a full circle
before it hits the water—that flashlight—
or 10-inch crescent wrench, or your cell phone
slipping out of your pocket as you bend down—
in the air before you know it.

It lands on the water's surface
like you land on the bed after a long day,
blankets fluffing, rising as they are displaced,
absorbing the impact and falling back again;
only the water receives and moves aside, and your knife,
the one you spent all those seasons sharpening,

the one you got in France years ago, on vacation—
a gift from the vendor who loved
that you were a commercial fisherman
and insisted you take it—is suddenly out of reach,
beneath the surface, fading, getting smaller and dimmer
as it recedes from you and all your memories of it,
out of your grasp forever in an instant,

like your friend who tipped over the edge after the struggle
to hang on to the rail while the disease rolled under her,
or the buddy who was brushed away in the morning light
when a car crested the hill and elbowed him into the air
before he knew it—a short fall into deep water.

Boat Fire

At first, the smoke is all we see,
a deep gray thread marring
a pure blue sky above the ache
of a calm sea. We spot it
at the same time, say,
Someone's on fire
just as the radio chatter begins.

A tin boat, one of the Carlson fleet—
guys are handing off extinguishers
to the skipper and crew, offering
to take them aboard if it gets too bad.
The smoke thickens, darkens to black,
billows. It isn't long before someone
says the two fishermen couldn't put
it out, and abandoned ship.

The boat is dead in the water,
burning as it drifts toward us,
turning a gorgeous day sour.
We pick up and move a mile away.
As we set the gear, a fireball blooms
above the stricken vessel but below the smoke,
rises high into the plume without a sound.

Gas tanks blew, a disembodied voice
clips on the CB a few minutes later,
but she didn't sink. The force of the blast
went upward, split her decks like a used
sardine can, but left her hull untouched.

When the Coast Guard skiff motors by
in the yellow light of evening, towing
her into the river, two figures sit, feet

over the side, orange survival suits peeled to waists,
shoulders slumped, eyes watching the water
slide past. Their hands hold cans of beer.
Someone at least was generous enough
to understand what they needed right then,
but though we watch them shrink into the distance,
we don't see either of them take a drink.

What Lingers

I read these poems and stories of the sea,
and you listen politely, but I can tell—
you look concerned.

Sounds dangerous, you say,
as you think of the television show
    Deadliest Catch
and what you've seen there.
But most fishing isn't like that at all.

When I tell stories
that sound death-defying,
too close for comfort or too close to call,
I rarely recall being touched by fear.

I never wanted
to scramble to the bow
while my broken-down boat
pitched and rolled in a heavy sea—
or sit, legs spread wide,
ass firmly planted on the trunk cabin
in order to have both hands free
so I could untie the anchor
and toss it over to keep us
from going on the rocks.

It was more of a problem to solve
than a fear to overcome.
Someone had to do it.

When my boat was heavy and low with fish,
and the engine quit in six-foot rollers,
Don tried towing me by tying alongside.
His deckhand bent over with a leg on each boat

and wrapped the line around my cleat just as
a swell slid under their vessel. The force of the sea
lifting his boat but not mine pulled on the cleat
with such force that its bolts, washers and nuts
slid up and through a two-inch-thick
oak plank like it was made of sea foam.
With a splash, the boats surged apart.

I saw his deckhand frozen with surprise
at the ocean's casual power and violence.
Without a thought I grabbed her
and pulled her on board.

No one remarked that I saved her life.
It was what had to be done.
There's no time to reflect during a moment like that.
You think about what happened once it's passed.
It occupies your mind while you drive away
from the cannery or toss back a shot at the bar;
you hope you continue to have the good sense
to make the right decisions that fast.

You hope the moment never gets too big
for your choices to continue to matter.

And if you're lucky
(because luck has a tremendous amount to do with it),
you'll make it through, and never look too deep
at how close you were to the edge.

But when telling the story years later,
what will surprise you
is how much the excitement lingers.

Sharp Knife

Reading fish stories
for the anthology I'm editing
is dancing with the past.
I whip around my office in gillnetters, power scows
and seine skiffs, wind in my hair and beard,
full of testosterone, not a fear on the horizon.

Packed with confidence built on youth, muscle
and bravado, I work on deck in fierce seas, pick fish
like raw meat, drink fifths of tequila, and tell myself
that cocaine is a legitimate fishing tool. I fall face-first
into the bunk each night for deep and dreamless sleep.

No need to dream. Tonight I dance at the bar
where fishermen go between openings, and we
close the place down. I shoot pool like a sharp knife,
fire potato-guns at beer cans out the back door,
and snort lines drawn out on a Devil's Club leaf.
My crew and I stink of salmon gurry and slime,
so we shower in our clothes and take a soggy cab
back to the boat.

§

When I finally come home, you aren't there.
The house is dark, your car isn't in the drive,
and to save my life, I have to figure out why.

Speck

Buck south against
the tide, twenty-knot wind,
cold rain, five-foot white-capping sea:
two more hours of this between us
and a school of fish we hope aren't
scattered by rotten weather.

Low ceiling, poor visibility;
spray fills the windshield.
We slam through the waves.
Sunrise colors the hulls
of the clouds a queasy yellow.
The cabin heater blows on my face.
I can't tell if I feel flushed because of it
or the day I'm having.

Teeth clenched, I wedge knees
against console, grip the wheel
with both hands. Cigarette ashes
fall in my lap. My coffee cup
swivels in a gimbaled holder: cold
liquid leans, levels out, leans again—
brown stains the carpet.

The radio barks, fills the cabin with static.
Inside a distorted squeal, a voice calls
my name: faint ghost of humanity
on another boat out here somewhere.
Electric bursts wrapped in white noise
pull me through the wire, reduce me
to pulses—ions emanating from
a twelve-foot whip antenna.

More static. My name again…
    Pick me up?
Another wave on the windshield.

I am a speck of a boat on big water—
  no one else in sight.

A Fishing Love Poem

Your heart,
the roar of an engine,
echoes through fathoms of me,
through wood, fiberglass and metal,
even my lead lining meant to muffle out noise.
I can't shake your presence—
275 turbo-charged horses running full-out,
next to me,

  solid,
    rhythmic,
      to the bone.

Salmon smell like money,
diesel like defeat:
don't want no diesel on my baby,
unless you're bleedin' the fuel filter
or fillin' the tanks.

Give me the scent of fish:
salmon slime and blood
fill my nostrils—
smell like winter in Hawaii,
a new radar, steak on the grill,
a camera lens or a pickup fresh off the lot.

The stronger the smell of fish
on my hands, my sleeves, my skin,
the more I want to strut it at the bar
before I come home and drop into your bed.
Wash it down with tequila and beer.
Kiss it off with loose, salty lips.

If only you understood dear,
and inhaled my salmon perfume
like the sweet cologne
of a wealthy man.

For today I am rich.
Today I own the sea. Today I own the fish.
Our boat and I left port empty and clean.
We return loaded with sockeye, gurry, and slime.
Both of us full.

Swim over here
and pick the scales from my beard, darlin'.
I fall into your arms, smellin' of all
the world's smells
   for you.

Twilight on the Boat

The last of the light
fades from the western sky
until the mountains melt into the dark.
We are rafted to six other boats
adrift on a gentle swell,
stopped on a school of salmon.

The scattered vessels of the fleet
are dark shadows in the distance—
white lights glimmer above them
as they drift south with the ebbing tide.
It's hard to tell where they stop
and the stars begin.

I sit on deck,
lean against the stack,
still warm from the run south
out of the river to beat the tide.
A seat cushion beneath me,
flashlight balanced on my shoulder—
reading, trying to wind down
the wire of nerves I always feel
before a big day.

Caught up in the story
I batten out the night noises:
the soft clinking of rigging moving
with the swell; the gurgles,
sloshes of the hulls,
the sigh of the sea so close.

A sound behind me—faint at first,
then again, and there, again,
a whoosh of an exhale   a breath
a gasp for air.

I put the book down and stand,
slow and quiet, to see first one
arcing shape break the surface next to me—
then another: a sliver of light gray
rising from black water.

Belugas! I whisper into the cabin
of my boat and another. Word spreads.
We gather in deep twilight on a dark sea,
stand silent as they rise for air
around us, hunting the salmon
we are stopped upon.

No one speaks.

The night swells around us—
a void above and below,
dark upon dark, sprinkled
with specks of distant suns,

and a meeting in between
where we float, and they swim.

Pompadour

Name the year that was especially good:
high price and fish fill the gear wherever
we set the net. We watch the bank account
grow ten grand a day. 1,100 sockeye one opening,
1,600 the next. The cocaine dealers make as much
as well-paid crew; park trailers in the yard
next to empty campers owned by fishermen too busy
to sleep. We're glad they do. Makes our dropping
a couple hundred a week into their pockets easier.
They even take trips with their best customers—
faux-deckhanding on fish days and providing free product.

Everyone knows. No one cares. Toot becomes a tool
for exhausted crews and cannery workers
spending 22-hour days on the slime line.
After a shift one night, Peggy naps in a pickup bed,
one leg hanging off the tailgate when a car backs into her.
She didn't do coke. Some of us think she should have.
At least she'd have been awake.

I run into town for supplies a few days later,
and collide with a lifelong dream:
chromed-out Honda Shadow 750,
parked in the grade-school lot across from the grocery.
She has the saddle seat lines of a vintage Harley,
a pompadour of a sign pinned to her handlebars—
FOR SALE: $3,000 or Best Offer. Leave message.
I use the pay phone outside the store.
We agree to meet when things slow down.
Planned in a cocaine haze, I don't mention it at home.

We use toot like raingear.
Put a line on the table
every time we pull on a jacket.

Suck lines into our noses
as we work rubber gloves onto our wrists.
Do a line running out the river,
before the first set,
before the first pick,
running on a fish call,
talking on the radio,
with coffee.
Stop for a bite almost never,
talk fast all day about anything,
about sex,
about more cocaine.

When we crash,
the lights don't just go out,
they blow.
Alarms blare,
we get up, do it again.
Absent at home, all I'm about
is heading to the boat
to catch more fish,
do more coke.

We sell to a cash buyer after one trip—
I jam crisp hundreds into a plastic grocery bag,
stuff it under the seat of my blue Ford pickup
parked in the cannery yard, then go out fishing
'til the end of the week. Once the reds run out,
I meet the bike's owner in town.

My ass in that saddle feels like a hand in a glove;
I hear the engine purr, go for a wind-in-my-hair ride—
never think once about how good my choices are.

I hand him the cash and drive home.
I already own the leather—

a black helmet with a skull,
my ensemble's complete.

Cocaine logic is the perfect solution
for the building seas of marital disaster:
30 one-hundred-dollar bills in an envelope,
her name on it. *Spend it any way you want, sweetie.*
You might anticipate how that worked out.
I don't.

She puts the money in the bank.

Name the year that was especially bad:
this is the low-water story of that summer.
I bump bottom with that bike, as off course
as Joe Hazelwood skippering the *Exxon Valdez*.

It takes me years to realize how lucky I am to miss the reef.

Under the Curve

We came upon her parked in the boneyard,
well away from the derelicts rotting on barrels,
boats that had seen their day chasing salmon,
riding the tides up and down the Inlet for decades,
now put to pasture in the weeds, stripped for parts,
oakum dripping from between the planks, and rust
streaking down the hulls from a thousand cuts.

She was wood too, but the load she carried
on her last trip was too much to bear. Just outside
the river mouth, she bumped the sandbar
at the bottom of a roller and popped a plank.
She made it to the shallows outside the channel
near shore before she went down. The crew escaped,
but she sat for a week until they could raise her.

They brought her to the cannery, lifted her out
with the travel lift, hydraulics straining under the load
of a waterlogged boat and fishhold full of seven-pound
sockeye—someone guessed over 2,000 of them.
The superintendent and his Beach Gang knew
what would come next, so they put her far from
where the fishermen and cannery grunts lived or worked.

We were experienced enough to know better, but didn't.
We fished a wooden boat, and the story of a blown plank
captured our imaginations and curiosity. Beers in hand,
we walked up the gravel road and down into the bowl
where she waited, silent, to be lit on fire after the appraisers
had their look. As we neared, the scene grew grim:
this was no derelict slowly slipping back into the grass.

She was dirty—rubbed raw dirty, like you feel as a kid
after you crash your bike in the gravel. Wounded.

The shape of her hull was off, her keel cracked, broken
under all that weight and a week of tides pushing at her.
But she was still intact, the way a car is still a car
after it's been totaled, and though she was beaten
and battered, she still looked like a boat.

We neared enough to see the small, perfect cone of white
beneath her and, not understanding, bent under the curve
of her hull to look closer, just when another maggot
dropped through the hole the plank had left behind
and landed on top of the growing pile.

The stench hit us like a caulking mallet, filling our nostrils,
our mouths and our throats with the scent of thousands
of dead fish carcasses. Gagging and swearing,
we threw our beers and ran.

We raced back to the cannery, where the smell of fish
meant money in our pockets, where disaster and death
weren't sleeping together, where the air, filled as it was
with the scent of salt, mud, diesel, and even salmon,
was still breathable.

It took hours to get that odor off our clothes,
out of our nostrils, off our tongues,
learning as we scrubbed that curiosity
isn't always a virtue.

Farewell

for the Skookum Too

She was my first boat,
a jerry-rigged derelict
with a sketchy past.
Perfect for a guy like me.

Never built to fish—
she was a wooden plug
used to make a form
for 32-foot fiberglass hulls.

But somewhere along the line
the company got greedy
and decided to sell her too.
Maybe that's where she got her name.

By the time I bought her from
the cannery, she'd been around
the yard more than a few years,
and looked it.

I got a deal, so I thought, because
her engine was pulled for a rebuild,
and the cannery guaranteed it to be
working before the season started.

But after dozens of years as a leased boat
with no preventative maintenance, and decades
of fixes addressing symptoms, not causes
of bigger issues, I was in for a bouncy ride.

Electrical, hydraulic, fuel, steering—every wire,
hose, a few planks in the hull, and damn near

every bolt would need to be upgraded
or replaced over the next eight years.

I was aboard when they installed her engine.
I was aboard as engineers hooked up her systems.

I added a flying bridge,
sister-ribbed the fishhold,
installed a new reel drive,
hydraulic motor and hoses,

new steering ram and controls,
new fuel tanks, filters and hoses,
new stove, new batteries, electronics,
wiring, water tank…and hoses.

What I didn't know
(which was pretty much everything),
I learned—not from YouTube or Google,
but from old-timers, experienced skippers and crew,

and fishermen friends who as a joke
locked me in the lazarette,
yet taught me how to tighten
the packing on a stuffing box.

By the time I sold her
to raise cash for a new boat,
she'd caught me tons of fish.
Ours had become a love/hate affair.

We knew each other's strengths
and failings. She brought me through
storms I didn't think she'd weather.
We'd seen each other at our worst

and at peaks of fishing proficiency
I never thought I'd attain.
The guy who bought her
fished for a different cannery.

Walking the dock in Ninilchik
a couple of years later,
I recognized her from a distance
like an old lover.

But when I got close, I saw
her paint was chipped and peeling.
Her sides were coated with rust.
I rested my hand on her gunwale

and apologized.

I never saw her again.
He ran her on the rocks
near the Barren Islands
and left her there.

None of us
gets to choose
how it ends,
only how it goes.

Buoys

I sit next to a darkened window on a windy night,
storm clouds casting a haze across my reflection
on black glass.

I want buoys to mark my way
like they did when I owned a boat.
Channel buoys that lean with the current:
red-and-green cans with wakes behind,
as if the buoys themselves are under way,
motoring over the muddy bottom, not anchored
with the tide doing all the work.

I point my bow between them,
follow the path they mark and trust
the heading. I leave navigation to engineers:
those who know the vagaries of the channel better than me,
whose study of currents, silt deposits and sandbars
tell them where the shifting hazards are,
and where to mark the course for the rest of us.
I notice each one as I pass, logging my voyage
by the numbers, in order, port and starboard,
green and red, bells, lights, whistles all in place.

If only life were that simple, that easy:
to steer a channel someone else dredged
and look out a black window at red-and-green lamps
reaching through the dark, blinking the way home.

The Old Man and the Sea Deal

You know the Hemingway story
The Old Man and the Sea, right?
Most of us do. Santiago, a grizzled fisherman,
hardened by years on the ocean,
goes out to deep water alone in his dory,
and hooks a monster marlin. The epic battle
between them lasts three days and nights,
wounds and exhausts them both.
He finally pulls the fish alongside and kills it
even as he admires it. But on the way home,
with the defeated, dead giant lashed to the boat,
he is discovered by sharks who rip his treasure
into ragged, bloody scraps. There's more, just not here
in this poem. Read the story. It's good.

Maybe this is the revenge tale: my last day
fishing—ever—in Cook Inlet after 20 years,
came and went without me realizing it.
On that day, I caught my second—ever—salmon shark.
A close relative of the great white, salmon sharks
are half the size of their large cousins. Teeth tangled
in my net like the first one I caught and released
a decade earlier, this one rang dollar signs in my head.
I decided to keep it, fetching a good price I thought,
for shark steak in local restaurants.

We pulled her on board with hydraulics.
She was a quarter ton of muscle and bad attitude
with a deck bucket of razors on the business end,
and a tail that could snap a man's leg on the other.
She thrashed when hoisted out of the water, frenzied jaws
snapping as she whipped and bucked. Once aboard,

she filled the stern while we moved out of the way.
She was remarkably calm when we slit her gills so she
would bleed out.

Imagine—a knife in the lung.

Had I remembered, I might have thought to say,
This is for Santiago. But I didn't.
Had I thought twice, I may have realized keeping her
meant ending her. *Just one among many*,
you might counter. *What's the big deal?*

The big deal was how she fought like Santiago's marlin.
How she was bigger than life, even in her last moments,
and the biggest deal was that it was mercenary.
That year sharks were everywhere in Cook Inlet.
The restaurants had been buying, but sales had slowed.
No one wanted her.

Except to teach me a lesson about greed, the deal was,
it was all for nothing.

It's Never the First

I spend the evening in pajamas
not in orange raingear with sleeves and boots
duct-taped to keep icy water from
soaking my hoodie, sweats and long
underwear as I pick Bering Sea crab
in February.

I switch on the family-room gas fireplace
with a click of a remote instead of working
an iced-over deck under orange sodium lights
in 11 degrees and choppy seas.

I recline in my easy chair, cat purring on footstool
next to the blanket wrapped round my legs.
I don't have to stop, turn my back,
brace against a wave crashing upon me,
threatening to slam me across the deck
or worse.

I pick up my iPad, play solitaire as the TV drones,
no sledge in hand cracking ice from the rigging,
rails and pots stacked 20 feet high, fighting
to keep the boat from getting top-heavy
in freezing spray.

I speak into the new TV remote: *Watch Jeopardy*,
and it automatically changes channels.
There was no time tonight for a microphone call
on the 98-foot crabber *Destination*.
The only way anyone knew she went down in the dark
off St. George Island was by an automatic signal
from an EPIRB they found the next day,
floating in an oil slick.

§

It's never the first one, one of their brothers said.
*They probably took a big wave that put them on their side,
then another and another.... The only ones who know
for sure are at the bottom of the ocean.*

Six people. Six fishermen at the rail, looking at a sunset
thinking of home, thinking about tomorrow.

Dust

for Louis Clark

Dust
doesn't care that we aren't here anymore—
that we don't sit on the boardwalk and bullshit
at mug-up, sip from Styrofoam cups,
laugh at the stupid things we do,
or frown at the way things go sometimes.

Sometimes
we dance on deck as bunch after bunch hits the net;
dance with the pretty deckhand at the bar after a shot.
When I stood on the stern and fired a shot
at a sea lion working my gear, I instantly wondered
how I let myself get to this.

This
was only about drinking whiskey at the bar
with the old-timer who had plenty to say
but not much time to say it. I asked you again
as I rubbed my eyes half an hour before closing,
One more story?

The story
wasn't ever about making money or competing
with other commercial guys, whether they were
on the line next to us, working setnets near shore,
or guiding six rods and reels in a crowded puker
up the river.

Up the river
the ones that get away still dig redds in the gravel,
lay their eggs and float downstream, rotting as they
continue to breathe; and they never do get away—
heartbeat at the end, to the very end of all of us,
nothing left but dust.

Dust
as dry as my mouth the morning after. Dust
that swirls in the wind, snakes its way off the gravel,
hovers before dropping to the river as it slides to sea,
pausing to glisten in morning's pale light
before it disappears.

Summer's Ebb

In Alaska the sun loses warmth well before it hits the horizon. The air turns cold above the water, and you'd best put on your flannel and turn up the stove, especially if you're running.

Once in the river, the sun takes its time going down—bow line tied to the stern cleat of the boat in front as you wait to deliver to the tender. You stand in the stern, catch the line of the boat pulling in behind you, tie it off and bullshit about the day. The conversations about weather, numbers of fish and breakdowns slow, then pause to watch as the sky stretches gold and the sun drops behind the roofs of the cannery. The horizon still shines bright when you look down, notice your empty hands and parched throat.

Cans dripping ice are pulled out of coolers, tossed like fish around the boats, between the boats and even over a boat into the river with a splash and a chorus of laughter. Unopened, it pops to the surface, floats downriver with the tide, crew after crew trying to dipnet it until someone yells at the skiff motoring by, and the underage kid at the helm chases down the runaway. He whips the skiff about to bring the beer back—you wave him off with a grin and shout, *That's yours!* He pops the can open in a spray of foam, raises it, twists the skiff around and takes a swig just as he bounces across his own wake. Froth showers his face. He wipes his chin with a sleeve, laughs and races away, a long shadow falling across the sides of the bigger boats, the wake rocking them, reminding everyone aboard that they aren't on solid ground even here, that this is not ordinary nor normal no matter how common or good it feels.

The beer warms and the cans are emptied. The talk dies and the tiredness of a day of heavy work and long hours seeps in. The sky mixes vermilion and violet and the last cloud finishes glowing; all that's left is a cold salt breeze that rattles the stove stack and reminds you of how swiftly summer slides out with the tide.

Where'd All the Fish Go?

for Don

Where'd all the fish go? Anybody know?
They were thick enough to walk on just a week ago.
We had jumpers in the air as far as we could see,
and nets filled with bonus trips to the cannery.

Where'd all the fish go? East? West? Uphill? Down?
Up north there's a bunch of tin boats runnin' around,
but there's nothin' I can spot, nowhere to be seen,
'cept whitecaps on the water and the gull's lonely scream.

The tide's comin' in—there should be a show—
on the flood the middle's where they usually go.
But there's nothin' here, not like yesterday.
Today the rip is empty. Like they just flew away.

They've gotta be somewhere, a guy on the CB just said,
but hell if I know which way to head.
That seems to be the story. It's the same east and west.
Sittin' here waitin'—drinkin' coffee seems best.

A boat down south saw some hits at opening today
and now half the freakin' fleet's chargin' hard his way.
Ya know, maybe the big slug of fish we dream of each fall
is finally comin' in—and we can get 'em all!

Jumpers a mile and a half wide and five miles long—
I got a pal who says he saw 'em, and he ain't often wrong.
But chasin' radio fish don't make much sense to me.
About all you ever catch is a net full of sea.

I don't know what else to do, so I pour another cup
and stand in the stern, lookin' out 'til I conjure up
a jumper in the hook and a splash in the net!
My crew likes the action—he's dancing on deck

and says a school might show; could be right, I suppose.
Guess I'll stay 'til there's a reason for the washdown hose.
I wonder if they've sounded, or'r swimmin' up the beach?
I could drop a net near shore, but I'd need someone to teach

me how to scoop 'em up without tearin' the gear.
Nah, instead I'll bounce around in deep water—out here.
Out here where there's no rocks or fish to be found.
Damn! I sure hope there's a few more sockeye around.

The few boats that do wait to call it a season
might catch that late run—after all, that's the reason
we stay—to fill our nets out here all by ourselves,
while the other boats sit on shore like books on shelves.

Wouldn't that be a hoot, though, to be out here in the fog
and load up on late reds, some silvers and dogs,
fill up the net and hold, then come in runnin' low?
And next year they'll ask—*Where DID you go?*

But you were alone when you nailed 'em all
so you don't have to tell 'em; didn't have to call
anyone on the radio as the boat got full.
You were busy pluggin' scuppers—sealin' the hull

and laughin' with your crew on a full fishhold high
with the stereo cranked and slappin' slimy high-fives,
while the fish just kept comin' on a silver rope
that carried you to glory, and gave the rest of us hope.

Snuffy

Day by day the old hull breaks apart,
planks soaked in seawater rot a little more
each time the tide floods. Paint blisters
and flakes away, worn by sun, wind,
ice, snow, rain. Scavengers scour
the bones looking for copper wire,
a cleat or a corroded brass fitting.

Summer after summer,
on the way to your own boat
you walk past her, beached
near the harbor. Occasionally
you notice the decline and wonder,
When did she get so old?

Eventually someone chainsaws
her cabin to use as a playhouse,
but the kids grow up and leave, and one day
a last weathered rib finally slips
from the beach with the outgoing tide.
It doesn't even leave a hole.

For years she never crossed your mind
until someone posts a photo on Facebook
and seeing it, you nod your head,
say, *I knew that boat.*

And the twenty or thirty or, fuck me,
forty years that are behind you
suddenly sit right on top of you—
a fishhold too full to float,
compressing your chest, making
each new wave harder to take.

Flash in the Distance

I am from gillnetters:
from the *Skookum Too* and the *Veronika K.*
I am boats floating a night sea,
raindrops on the back of a wave.

I am from salmon slime, flake ice, scales and gurry.
I am hissing stick rips, glassy seas,
wild-horse, white-maned wave stampedes.

I am *waterhaul* and *roundhaul*, radio fish
and sunken nets; clatters, splashers,
nudgers, jerkers, *nothing much*
and *better get over here right away.*

I am from beer on the back deck,
baseball caps, flotation vests and rubber boots.
I am Grundens, XtraTufs, Vickies, and Stormy Seas.

I am where sunrise ignites the sea,
volcanoes vent over the island,
Belugas rise to greet stars.

I am needles of rain on my cheeks,
salt spray on the windshield,
the shuddering slam of the hull.

I am a fire in the cabin, a blown fan belt,
oil in the bilge, catching a line from a tender for a tow.

I am a flash in the distance, whitecaps in the rip,
bow slicing an ocean swell, foam in my wake.

First Net

The car idles and waits roughly for the stoplight:
the smell of oil and hot grease fills my nostrils;
    I am lifted to a world of boats,
        engines
            and fish.

Days, weeks, months: seasons of my life
have been spent smelling this odor and fixing boats,
    trying to get this part or that off or on,
    struggling to reach dropped bolts in the bilge,
        twisting into contorted positions
            to get that extra purchase to turn a fitting just so.

    On these forsaken vessels
I have designed, puzzled and planned;
fabricated, rebuilt, retooled, and forsworn;
sanded, painted, gel-coated, welded and fiberglassed.
    I have cut, torn, pounded, lubricated, sawn,
     screwed, rasped, nailed, bolted, lashed,
    scraped, scoured, drilled, filled
        and cursed.

I have come home coated in thick grease,
soaked in diesel, sticky with silicone, crusty with Bondo,
    with resin in my hair.
I have felt the pride of looking at my hands as they dripped blood,
    laughed in surprise at strips of my own scraped-off skin,
wore calluses like badges, and danced with the sweet sting of cuts
    to the beat of scrubbing the dirt from under my nails—
    wondering if they would ever come clean again.

§

But I have watched all the long weeks of work, grime and wounds
    melt into sweet memory
        when the first net of the season
            hit the water.

I Have a Question

Does this poem breathe air
laced with salt
as you stand on deck
staring into a breezeless night,
the sea rolling beneath you?

Does it make you recall the smell of diesel
mixed with a faint fish odor in the bilge,
and how cramped and twisted you had to be
to break loose the rusted bolt
from its prison?

Does this poem make you remember
how it felt to run into a wild sea
to get to the fish? How the bow
pounded into the waves, spray spattering
the windshield, ramping up
your sense of urgency?

Have I crafted enough detail
here on this page to push you back
to days when climbing an outrigger
to free a tangled line while the sea raged
seemed reasonable,
necessary?

Would you risk it all for another brailer
of fish? Or did you never consider
this land-based question?
You never thought the one
who fell overboard
would be you.

What would you have this poem do?
It can't bring you back.
But it can remember:
an orange-and-ochre sunset,
a black-and-blue storm front,
a billion stars blazing above you.

Fat City in Four Directions

for Jeannie Ouren

    North
We thought we'd all be highliners.
 Each trip out we had visions of plugging the boat.
 We would sink the gear, and tie floats to the corkline
 so we could get the net back on board after it filled
 with sockeye. We'd call a tender to off-load us while fresh
 flurries frothed the water's surface. We'd roundhaul
 the final set, deck loaded and the boat so low we'd toss
 the last of the catch into the cabin or put 'em in net bags
 and drag 'em to the bow to balance the load. We'd fly
 a broom from the rigging as we returned to the river.

 We were on course to Fat City.

    South
On the way, we bucked into stiff winds and big tides.
 We ran over each other's gear in the glare of the sun
 on steel-gray waves and ended up dead in the water
 with web in the wheel. Engine alarms blared as we blew
 alternators and threw fan belts. We spent frantic hours
 jerry-rigging spare parts so we could stay on the grounds.
 We swore at our misfortune as reports of big catches and
 fresh hits spat frustration out of tinny deck speakers;
 we turned off the radio before it described more fish calls
 we couldn't get to.

We stood adrift in the stern, watching
 even as the best catches of the season moved into the
 river. The rip sucked us into the sticks or the kelp,
 and a faulty solenoid or water in the fuel had us catching
 a line from the tender that would tow us home empty.

East
Some days we'd just flat-out not find 'em:
   move east when they showed on the west side,
   stop running a mile short of where they'd pop up,
   or set a net length too far from the rip.
   Worse, they wouldn't be there at all:
   we'd spend the day scratch fishing while radio fish
   filled imaginary nets and the hits weren't the bunches
   we expected, just singles, or only a surface show.
   The talk would turn to escapement policies of Fish and
   Game, and how the biologists, politicians and guides
   were killing us. The only fish on board were headed
   for the freezer at home.

West
Some of us
   still weather low prices and less fish:
   In the cold morning dawn silhouettes of boats
   still glide past closed canneries and derelict docks.
   On board, skippers still hold a coffee mug in one hand
   and steer the boat down a darkened river with the other.
   Deckhands still coil lines in the stern and scan the sea
   for jumpers.

But some of us put the boat on barrels and sold the permit.
   Cleaned out our lockers, packed the trailers
   and pulled away in a cloud of dust.
   No more waves to lift us.
   Instead, we steer through the changing currents
   of foreign seas: oceans of commerce and business.
   We ride the ebb and swell of the job market,
   negotiating interviews like we used to quarter the boat
   through heavy weather.
   We still run hard, looking for jumpers.

   We still search for Fat City.

Microphone

Resting next to you tonight,
listening to your rhythmic sleep,
I key the marine radio microphone
and set the channel to twenty years ago.
Skookum Too, Skookum Too, I whisper,
    Pick me up?

I release the button to a short burst of white noise,
and wait, listening, while the smell of salt air
fills my mind. I feel the boat lift as a wave rolls under me,
hold the mic close again: *Yeah, the Skookum Too,*
    you pick me up there, Pat?

I don't know what I'm thinking.
I have something to say to the me riding rough weather
in an old wood boat, wishing I was somewhere else.
Something to offer a young man with high hopes
    and an empty fishhold.

But the radio stays silent,
and wondering if it still works, I turn down the gain
until static erupts from the speaker like fire.
I roll the dial back again, stop on the other side of silence.
I know he's out there, face flushed, burning from the inside,
    too caught up in the moment to appreciate it.

So I try once more to raise him,
and though I think I hear a voice,
faint and unclear, it's something that blurs,
like looking through salt spray on the windshield
    or a whisper that echoes as you awaken from a dream.

I blink as the reverie fades.
The night deepens, the voice slips away.
I give it up, drop the microphone and reach out to you.
A soft moan from a dream of your own escapes your lips
    and hangs, ringing in the dark.

View from the Stern

Often I stood on the back deck
of my boat, legs working

like pistons as she rolled forward
and aft, port to starboard.

Some days that dance required more
work. When the breeze freshened,

it would send a thrill mixed with
apprehension to tighten my chest.

More than once I stood wide-eyed
as I watched a front move up the inlet—

a dark-cloud curtain. Reports of building seas
turned excitement to dread. We picked gear, frantic

as fear rose with the wind's song in the rigging,
only to find our imaginations were far fiercer

than most storms. Rather than run home with tails tucked,
we stayed and rode it out. Other fish days, long gone

to me now, the ocean offered up magical reflections
on glassy water and a slight swell coming in with the flood.

Wherever I would look, moving lines of light rolled off
dark water, merged with dark lines floating on light.

I'd pause, mesmerized instead
of watching fish hit the net, and wonder:

How did I get to be so lucky?

Someone once asked me, *What's it like, working on the water for a living?*

Mending Holes

for Lee

I touched the past
   even as it disappeared before me.
   I placed my hands upon the backs of hours
   loaded heavy with gear,
   and pushed them down an elevated boardwalk
      toward oblivion.

I mended holes in the days
   with a needle and twine;
   swatted mosquitoes like seconds
   as summers sped beneath me.
   I painted coats of the present
   upon planks of history,
   then years later spent months of chainsaws
   cutting them into pieces,
   then bulldozing them onto the beach
   where I lit the match that burned them to ashes.
      I even hoisted a beer in their honor.

I've seen compasses lose direction,
   watched a fleet of seasons sink over the horizon;
   seen sail give way to power,
   wood give way to glass;
   species disappear under thick coats of oil,
      and lifestyles vanish beneath politicians' dark coats.

I pulled decades of tradition onto shore,
   put them on barrels
   and walked away, leaving them to decay.
   Winter storms weakened them.

Summer sun bleached them,
and I returned years later
    to feel them crumble between my fingers.

What my eyes have forgotten
  my hands remember:
  cool, wet cotton gloves,
  stiff, rough, manila line
  and the heavy chains of anchors
    covered in generations of mud.

§

I lean into the cool plastic of this buoy:
  like seconds into hours
  it gives before resisting,
  and reminds me
  that ebbing times,
  with all the gear,
    work,
      and fish,
  are like a boat on a set in a strong tide:
  from on board all we see is the set;
  but from anywhere else,
  the boat and net grow smaller
    as they drift into the distance.

Writing About Fishing

My eyes burn.
I don't want to write about it anymore…
   I want to fish.

I don't want to celebrate beautiful mornings
on water like glass with marks on paper;
or wax dramatic on a keyboard about rough
weather, surviving despite the odds—all the gods
watching, lined up along the shore
   taking bets on whether I live or die.

I want to wave a fist at them from the bridge,
defy their wagers in orange raingear,
ride the boat into the teeth of the best they can heave.
I want to step onto the dock filled with insolence:
a shot of Cuervo in one hand,
   a belly laugh in the other.

I don't want to write about
how much I miss the sea when I'm stuck on land;
how the smell of salt and a seagull's cry
pull an ache out of my chest. I want to
set boot to deck and wrench open the door
   to the great adventure!

I'll endure the froth or else sink like the stone
you'll carve my name into on shore,
where I find myself forever
   not wanting to write about it.

Exit Strategy

I shall leave today,
motor through a school of leaping fish
stretched from the river mouth
to the horizon's soft curve,

sluice my bow through green
ocean swell, tide on my stern,
sun white alongside, burning
reflection in a moving mirror.

I will walk eternity
on salt water, flesh food
for crab, blood thick brine,
bones ground to sand.

Find me in the wave's roll,
riding a flash of silver
bound for home, bound for the river
where the Great Bear feasts fat
in the howling wind, shaking
the crash of life from the breaking surf
caught in his jaws at the edge of the sea.

I depart on Raven's wings,
black night above boats adrift
waiting for the coming day—
I fly toward stars that rise
dripping from the deep,
my ragged caw echoing ahead,
faint in the distance.

Acknowledgments

I'm grateful to the editors of the journals, anthologies, and magazines that first gave the following poems water to swim within:

Alaska Fisherman's Journal: "Fat City in Four Directions"

Anchored in Deep Water (anthology): "Some Fourth of Julys"

Cirque: "Boat Puller," "Overboard," "Sextant"

FISH 2015 (anthology): "Flash in the Distance"

Like Fish in the Freezer (anthology): "Middle Rip"

North Pacific Focus: "Pompadour" (as "Best Offer"), "Mending Holes"

Gratitude

I've been lucky to have a wife like Veronica Kessler, sharing her love, support, and invaluable critique as these poems were lived, written, revised, and assembled into this collection. It's been a journey of almost 50 years, and though we've had rough weather, you've been there when I needed it the most. This book is as much yours as it is mine.

I have a deep appreciation for a boatload of fishermen who took a risk and supported me on the fishing grounds, especially Thor and Jim Evenson and Dean and Don Pugh. I'd also like to thank the small but enormously important raft of readers I've had for many years, who have offered their gentle advice and critique on the hundreds of poems I have floating in my wake: Marc Berezin, Erin Fristad, Doug Ford, and Holly Hughes. My writers' groups have been invaluable in making certain my poems were crafted to the best of my ability, among them my friends Wes Jones, Joanne Clarkson, Thomas A. Thomas, Bridgit Lacy, Carol Sunde, and Terri Cohlene. I am fortunate to be on the Olympia Poetry Network board. It and its members have also been supportive and encouraging upon hearing my work at the open mics. And finally, my deepest gratitude for the FisherPoets Gathering for welcoming me into their fold nearly 30 years ago, at a time when I desperately needed a community and family to be a part of. First and foremost, I am a fisherpoet.

I cannot state emphatically enough how grateful I am for the support and understanding of MoonPath Press's Managing Editor, Lana Hechtman Ayers. She's held my hand throughout this process with kindness, encouragement, and clarity. She is the type of editor every author hopes for. It has been an absolute delight to work with her. I also appreciate the hard work and beautiful eye of Tonya Namura, MoonPath's design magician.

Last but certainly far, far from least, I must express my love and heartfelt thanks to my sister and brothers, Judy, Jim and Mike, and especially to my two sons Kessler and Dylan, their partners in life, and my grandchildren for their support and joy, making this the best, most complete life I can imagine.

About the Author

Patrick Dixon is a writer/photographer retired from careers as an educator and commercial fisherman. A member of the board of directors of the Olympia Poetry Network, he has been published in several literary journals, including *Cirque, Claudius Speaks, Linden Avenue, Mom Egg Review, Oberon, Panoplyzine, The Raven Chronicles, Soul-Lit, The Tishman Review*, and *World Enough Writers* among others. His work appeared in the anthologies *Examined Life, The Madrona Project #7, FISH 2015,* and *WA 129*. He was included in the Washington State Book Award–winning anthologies *Take a Stand: Art Against Hate* (Raven Chronicles, 2020) and *I Sing the Salmon Home* (Empty Bowl, 2024).

Mr. Dixon is a past poetry editor of *National Fisherman* magazine's quarterly, *North Pacific Focus*. A member of the FisherPoets Gathering organizing committee, he received an Artist Trust grant to edit *Anchored in Deep Water: The FisherPoets Anthology* (2014). His chapbook *Arc of Visibility* won the 2015 Alabama State Poetry Society Morris Memorial Award. His poem "Western Washington November" was selected as a winner of the 2023 "Poems of Place" competition by *Cirque* literary journal. His poem "Twilight on the Boat" and photograph "Dancing Sky" were selected by the Alaska Department of Parks and Outdoor Recreation for an interpretive sign at Bird Point Park, a beluga whale viewing spot south of Anchorage along the Seward Highway.

Mr. Dixon spent his childhood in Logansport, Indiana, but grew up when he moved to Kenai, Alaska in 1975, where he lived for 23 years. *Mending Holes* is his first full-length collection of poetry.

www.ingramcontent.com/pod-product-compliance
Lightning Source LLC
LaVergne TN
LVHW041539070526
838199LV00046B/1744